What's Inside a
Firehouse?

Sharon Gordon

BENCHMARK BOOKS

MARSHALL CAVENDISH
NEW YORK

Inside a Firehouse

1. beds
2. computers
3. garage
4. kitchen

5 ladder truck
6 meeting room

7 pumper truck
8 turnout gear

Fire! The *dispatcher* takes the call.

The alarm in the nearest firehouse rings loudly. It calls the firefighters to action. The firehouse *siren* goes on.

In many small towns, the firefighters are *volunteers*. They also have other jobs.

These firefighters rush to the firehouse when their pagers start beeping.

Everything the firefighters
need is at the firehouse.
The fire trucks are inside
the garage.

Special clothes called *turnout gear* are kept nearby. Tools, such as chainsaws and *generators*, are ready to use.

Big cities pay firefighters to stay at the firehouse day and night.

In between calls, the firefighters work on the trucks. They check the supplies and make repairs.

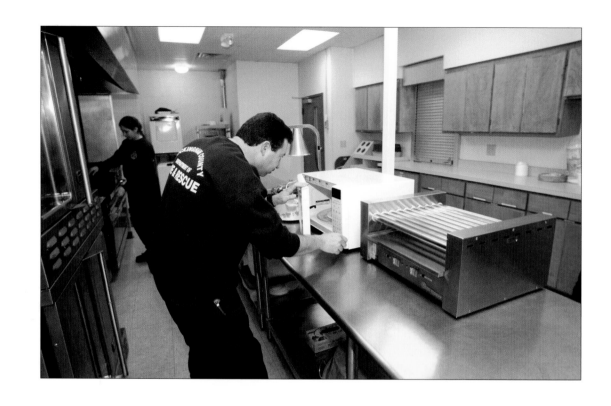

The firehouse is like their home.
There is a kitchen for cooking
and eating.

The firehouse has desks with computers and a large room for meetings. It even has beds for sleeping.

But there is no time to sleep now!

The firefighters jump to their feet and run. It is time to gear up.

Turnout gear protects the firefighters from the heat and flames. These pants and jackets are very heavy.

High rubber boots protect the firefighters' feet. *Helmets* and heavy leather gloves protect their heads and hands.

The firefighters work as a team. They are ready to go in seconds.

They lift the garage doors. They take their places on the trucks. Off they go!

There are ladder trucks and *pumper* trucks inside the firehouse.

The pumper is usually the first to leave. It can pump water from its own tank or from nearby *fire hydrants*.

The ladder truck is good
for reaching tall buildings.

Sometimes there is a big
bucket on top of the ladder.
It helps the firefighters rescue
trapped people and animals.

Sometimes, the fire is too big for one fire department to handle. The fire chief calls for help on his two-way radio.

Other firehouses send their firefighters to help. They work together until the fire is out.

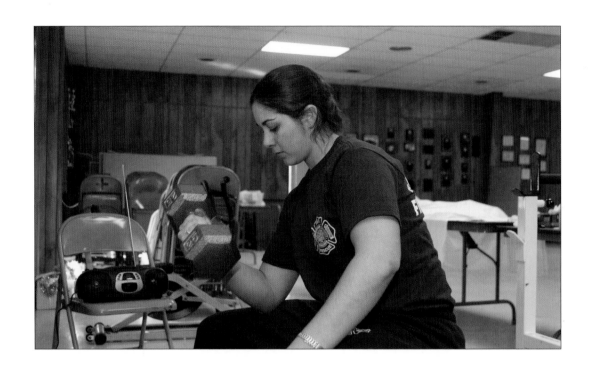

Back at the firehouse, the firefighters take a break. They can watch television or exercise.

But then another bell rings. The
firefighters jump to their feet.
It is the dinner bell. Time to eat!

Challenge Words

dispatcher—A phone operator who takes emergency calls for the police, ambulance, and fire stations.

fire hydrant (high-drunt)—A metal pipe on the edge of a sidewalk that is connected to the main water supply.

generator (jen-uh-ray-tur)—A machine that produces electricity.

helmets—Strong hats that protect firefighters from heat and falling objects.

pumper—A fire truck that carries and pumps water.

siren (sigh-run)—An electrical horn that makes a loud up-and-down warning sound.

turnout gear—Heavy jackets and pants that protect firefighters from the heat and flames.

volunteer—A person who does a job without pay.

Index

Page numbers in **boldface** are illustrations.

With thanks to Nanci Vargus, Ed.D.
and Beth Walker Gambro, reading consultants

ACKNOWLEDGMENTS
With thanks to the men and women of the Grottoes, Virginia,
Volunteer Fire Department, Rockingham County Fire and Rescue

Benchmark Books
Marshall Cavendish
99 White Plains Road
Tarrytown, New York 10591-9001
www.marshallcavendish.com

Library of Congress Cataloging-in-Publication Data

Gordon, Sharon.
What's inside a firehouse? / by Sharon Gordon.
p. cm. — (Bookworms: What's inside?)
Includes index.
Summary: An introduction to life at a fire department, including
descriptions of the equipment, the staff, and what happens when a fire alarm goes off.
ISBN 0-7614-1562-9
1. Fire stations—Juvenile literature. [1. Fire departments.] I.
Title. II. Series: Gordon, Sharon. Bookworms. What's inside.

TH9148.G663 2003
628.9'25—dc21
2003006190

Photo Research by Anne Burns Images

Cover Photo by Jay Mallin

All of the photographs used in this book were taken by and used with the permission of Jay Mallin.

Series design by Becky Terhune

Printed in China
1 3 5 6 4 2